A Heroic Crown
and Other Sonnets

Collected Sonnets from
2020 - 2022

by
Paul Gilliland

A Heroic Crown

and Other Sonnets

Collected Sonnets from
2020-2022

by Paul Gilliland

A Heroic Crown and Other Sonnets

By Paul Gilliland

First Edition

Author: Paul Gilliland
Editor: Zoubida Roberts
Formatting: Southern Arizona Press
Cover Art: *King Arthur* by Charles Ernest Butler, 1903

Published by Southern Arizona Press
Sierra Vista, Arizona 85635
www.SouthernArizonaPress.com

ISBN: 978-1-960038-00-5

Poetry

Contents

Presented in the order written

The Tropical Zodiac Sonnets

The Chinese Zodiac Sonnets

Explanation of Sonnet Forms

His Bunkie
Drawing by William James Aylward, 1918

I

To Veterans
(English Sonnet)

They spend their youth in far off distance lands
and holidays are spent away from home.
They make a bed 'neath dunes of drifting sands
or underneath a bombed-out palace dome.
A duty to defend the country's call
with loyalty unto their brotherhood.
In honor proudly standing straight and tall
to sacrifice themselves for greater good.
This life is what these heroes chose to serve
for greatness is among the ranks of these.
The highest praise is what these few deserve
for life to them is but a day to seize.
And so, we give our thanks to every vet
for sacrifices we will not forget.

12 October 2020 [1, 5]

II

A Halloween Sonnet
(English Sonnet)

The witch and warlock make a clever brew
while ghosts and ghouls prepare the nightly feast.
This festive time comes once a year tis true
for 'morrow all the parties will have ceased.
The goblins bring the music for the dance
and Jack gives us an evil pumpkin smile.
For Dracula will put all in a trance
and things will be quite somber for a while.
The cauldron's fire reaches to the skies
as Dead and Gone join in the mummy's curse.
Then Frankie's monster will begin to rise
from in the wooden coffin in the hearse.
All hallows' eve is quite the party scene.
To all we wish a spooky Halloween.

12 October 2020 [1]

III

A Christmas Sonnet
(English Sonnet)

At night, the children hang each sock with care
and leave a plate of cookies and some tea.
In hopes that Santa Claus will visit there
and leave them stacks of presents 'neath the tree.
Their parents know this year that times were tight,
but do the best to give what they desire.
They've tried to save enough throughout this plight
to fill the stockings hung above the fire.
Three presents for each child are what's at hand.
A shirt, some socks, and shoes, and just one toy.
They pray the kids are pleased and understand
in hopes it brings each one some Christmas joy
and they won't measure love by what was spent
but rather by the gift that God has sent.

27 October 2020 [1]

IV

Two Roads Diverged
(English Sonnet)

Two roads diverged within a yellow wood
and sorry I could not explore them both
I looked down one as far off as I could
to where it disappeared amidst the growth.
But then, I took the other just as fair.
Perhaps, because it had a better claim.
For it was grassy, begging for some wear,
but passing there had worn then both the same
For neither road had leaves upon the clay.
Yet knowing not if I should e'er return,
I kept the first to hike another day.
I shall be telling you what I did learn.
Two roads diverged with a wood and I –
I took the one that seemed less traveled by.

– Based on the poem "The Road Not Taken" by Robert Frost

3 November 2020 [1]

V

Stopping by Woods
(English Sonnet)

Whose pine filled woods are these I think I know.
His house is in the village down below.
I'm sure he would not give a care, although
I sit to watch these woods fill up with snow.
My little horse must think it rather queer
To stop without a barn or stable near.
Although we hear the church bells ringing clear
On this, the darkest evening of the year.
My horse, he gives his harness bells a shake
To ask me if there must be some mistake
For stopping by the woods and frozen lake
Amidst the blowing wind and snowy flake.
For I have many promises to keep
And several miles to go before I sleep.

– Based on the poem "Stopping by Woods on a Snowy Evening" by Robert Frost

3 November 2020 [1]

VI

Fire and Ice
(English Sonnet)

Some say the world will end in burning fire,
the cleansing flames that signal a new birth.
For what I've tasted of my own desire,
I'd wish this ending to my life on earth.
Some say the world will end in freezing ice.
Though I would hold with those who favor fire.
For when that time doth come it may be nice
to end it on a blazing funeral pyre.
But if it comes that I should perish twice.
I think I've seen enough of worldly hate.
It may be best to hope for freezing ice
to seal me in a final frozen state.
Though some say they prefer the freezing ice
I think the burning fire would more suffice.

– Based on the poem "Fire and Ice" by Robert Frost

7 November 2020 [1]

VII

We Are Americans
(Acrostic English Sonnet)

With all the times that we might disagree
Each word and thought we speak to change one's mind

Although our plans are clear and plain to see
Replies to other's thoughts are hard to find.
Examples sometimes make our points more clear

And often we can see the other's side.
Moreover, when we take the time to hear
Explaining differences is bona fide.
Remember each is dealt a different hand
In troubled times we all must do what's right.
Cannot let party lines divide our land
As we all come together and unite.
Not Democrats or staunch Republicans
Since in the end, we're all Americans.

8 November 2020 [1]

VIII

The Rainbow
(English Sonnet)

The rain clouds had begun to fade away.
The wind was wisping them across the sky.
As rays of sun came poking out to play
the colors of the rainbow caught my eye.
As red and orange and yellow stood out bright,
the arc of many colors slowly grew.
The purples barely came into my sight
and green just faded in the sky of blue.
I stopped to watch it arch across the sky
with brilliant colors bright in every hue.
But then the colors that had caught my eye,
began to slowly vanish out of view.
The rainbow was a momentary gift
that God above had sent, my soul to lift.

8 November 2020 [1]

IX

Tales on Autumn Nights
(English Sonnet)

The cloudless skies of mid-November nights
form ceilings for forgotten tales of old.
As stars above provide the Heavens' lights
illuminating stories being told.
The legends told of heroes' quests for good
near fire lit to warm each hearth and home.
Where air that's filled with scents of burning wood
is mixed with crispness of the twilight gloam.
The children gather round to hear the tales,
some humorous and others filled with dread.
From romance on the sea in search of whales
to fantasies that fill each tiny head.
This is the time when family unites
to share their tales on chilly autumn nights.

11 November 2020 [1]

X

Man In the Mirror
(Acrostic English Sonnet)

My life has always been to be the best
And I know that is far from being true
No matter how my life's put to the test

I find the winning far between and few
Now triumph should not be my only goal

There comes a time when failure builds esteem
However, it can burn deep in the soul
Establishing one's name becomes a dream

May people all around me understand
I do not wish for only praise and fame
Reflecting on my life is now at hand
Recalling deeds brings credit to my name
Of all the good times held deep in my heart
Reflecting on those is the place to start

26 November 2020 [1]

XI

Changing Places
(English Sonnet)

Let us change places for a length of time.
Where opposite in rank we will remain.
For I will be the scholar, you the swine
and now in life I'll hold you in disdain.
I'll dine on caviar and fine French wine
and have the newest phone on which to call,
While you will eat the slop fed to the swine
and scratch your number on a bathroom wall.
For you, the dress will not keep out the cold,
while I'll be warm within my castle walls
and you will have no family to hold
while huddled in the dampness of the halls.
I'd like to change my life with you one day
but it would surely be to your dismay.

9 December 2020 [1]

– Inspired by the poem "Change, Changing Places" by Lori Regina Gilliland (1984) [3]

XII

(not) A Christmas Sonnet
(English Sonnet)

The room is dark and spinning all around
into an Advent wreath which should be lit.
With colored paper scattered 'bout the ground
beneath a tinseled tree that lists a bit.
Small figurines all cast in porcelain
in shrouded tissue, crumpled up and ripped,
awaiting visits from gift bearing men
remain encased inside their cardboard crypt.
The table sits with bowls piled high with food
upon a tablecloth of grandma's lace
where unlit candles fail to set the mood,
a golden turkey takes its center place.
As children run about the house and play
they've all forgot the meaning of this day.

9 December 2020 [1]

– Inspired by the poem "(not) A Christmas Sonnet" by Lori Regina Gilliland (1984) [3]

XIII

Caramel Popcorn
(Acrostic English Sonnet)

Come one, come all, the circus is in town!
Amazing acts from jugglers to trapeze
Ring two we see the funny smiling clown
An entertainer who is sure to please
Make way, here comes the elephant parade
Enjoy the music of the circus bands
Look left, look right, to see how dreams are made

Performers here from many different lands
Open your eyes, don't want to miss the mirth
Presented now to give you all a smile
Come one, come all, the greatest show on earth
Observe the entertainment for a while
Remember when the circus came to town?
Nobody ever dreamed they'd shut it down.

16 December 2020 [1]

25

XIV

Revolution
(English Sonnet)

A revolution's in the minds of some
but do they truly know of what they ask.
And where are these ideas coming from,
is it a puppet master in a mask?
Is what they seek to transform the regime,
dramatic changes in our very state?
Is this the realization of a dream
or something that has festered due to hate?
Or do they simply long for the rebirth
of systems they remember from the past?
A time that they recall upon the earth
when power in their favor was amassed.
Is revolution meant to change the view
or go back to the way that they once knew?

16 December 2020 [1]

XV

For My Muse, Euterpe
(English Sonnet)

Are you as gorgeous as a summer's day
when flowers bloom because of morning's dew?
Shall I expect that in the end you'll stay
or will you fade away into the blue?
Will waves upon the sand erode the shell
that echoes all the voices of the sea?
Will memories of you lead me to hell
and will they haunt me for eternity?
Or will the thoughts of your most loving glance
breathe life into my soul for all of time
while visions of your eyes instill a trance
that fills my lines of poetry with rhyme?
For as you guide me in my daily chore
I know you are my muse and nothing more.

20 December 2020 [1]

XVI

The Great Conjunction
(Couplet Sonnet)

A great conjunction's in the western sky,
as Jupiter and Saturn catch our eye.
Is this the sign that things on earth will change,
or only that they'll slightly rearrange?
But since the winter solstice is this day
the Great Conjunction will show us the way
for new advancements in technology,
in social issues, and authority.
As we begin Aquarian's new age
the next upcoming month should quell the rage
and since the planet Mars is in prograde
we all shall see the turmoil start to fade.
As these two planets start their cosmic run
a glint of hope in twenty twenty-one.

20 December 2020 [1]

XVII

To a Man Growing Old
(English Sonnet)

Oh ye, once youthful as a springtime sprout
that bloomed with warm embrace of sun-drenched rays.
For in your youth, you frolicked without doubt
that life would bring you fame and words of praise.
Oh ye, then handsome as a summer's day
and strong as ivory cliffs against the sea.
You dedicated life to work and play
with little thought of your mortality.
Oh ye, the grown mature and sought out sage
whose knowledge brought enlightenment to youth.
Who seek out all the wisdom of your age
and look to you for never-ending truth.
As winter slumber nights now call your name
you close your eyes to finish out life's game.

23 December 2020 [1, 8]

XVIII

Your Breath is Calming Like a Springtime Breeze
(English Sonnet)

Your breath is calming like a springtime breeze
that comforts both the body and the soul.
The broken hearts in pain you do appease
from gifted love so meaninglessly stole.
Your breath becomes the drying summer wind
of tears that fall like warm midsummer rain
upon the cheeks of angels who have sinned
while you appease the broken hearts in pain.
Your breath appears as cold gusts in the fall
that bring a chill and shiver down the spine.
The warmth of spring the memories recall,
appeasement of the broken hearts of time.
You rustle through the autumn's fallen leaves
and warm the hearts on frozen winter eves.

23 December 2020 [1]

XIX

The Rapture of the Newly Fallen Snow
(English Sonnet)

The quarter moon shines down without a sound
as downy flakes of snow begin to fall
to form a pure white blanket on the ground.
A peacefulness of which I can't recall.
The moon shine gives a luster to the chaste
and pureness of the untouched virgin white.
Creating magic scenes all inter-laced
translucent in the ever-changing night.
But as the wind blows swiftly 'cross the fields
and drives the snow to drift along the trees,
it proves the strength and power that it yields
to do with virgin flakes how e'er it please.
The rapture of the newly fallen snow
below the twinkling stars and soft moon glow.

26 December 2020 [1]

XX

Oh Ye, With Little Care for Things I Do
(English Sonnet)

Oh ye, with little care for things I do
with thoughts that all my time is put to waste.
Successes I achieve may be a few,
but all my hard work will not be erased.
The lines I craft may bring some folks a tear,
but my intention never was adverse.
I try to state each rhyme precise and clear
by keeping all my thoughts succinct and terse.
To you who wish me luck before my face,
but to my back your evil eye is cast
my constant work will put you in your place
for my success will leave you all aghast.
So, when you ask what farce I do today,
I'll rid your cynicism from my way.

27 December 2020 [1]

XXI

Jack Frost's Nightly Art
(English Sonnet)

The briskness of a January morn
when rays of sun are slow to break the day
reveal the frosted windows that were born
throughout the night when Jack was left to play.
Each morning's breath is filled with air so clean;
invigorating life among the old.
The glow of embers lingering between
the frosted glass of nighttime's winter cold.
For as the sun begins to warm the air
and temperatures outside begin to rise,
our dear friend Jack retires in the glare
of light infused throughout his frosted guise.
We stay to watch the breaking of the dawn
until the art of Jack is all but gone.

5 January 2021 [2, 4]

XXII

A Place to Take a Knee
(English Sonnet)

Our heroes in this hallowed ground are laid
In their eternal rest for all of time.
We honor them for sacrifices paid
Each given for our country in their prime.
We don't see different colors for the dead.
The headstones in this field all look the same.
There is no black or brown; no white or red,
The only true distinction is the name.
We do not see their race or know their creed
For this was not important to their task.
They served and helped each soul they found in need
And no request was e'er too much to ask.
Since color, race, and creed you cannot see
This is the place where we shall take a knee.

24 January 2021 [5, 9]

XXIII

A Storm Brewing at Sea
(Eramonian Sonnet)

The lonely lighthouse keeper watches west from top his keep,
for miles he sees the calming waves upon the vast blue deep.
Where setting sun reflects upon the sea like diamonds cast
and ships and boats of every size are slowly sailing past.
But as the weather changes and the sea begins to rise
he sees the dark clouds brewing up a storm before his eyes.
He goes into the lantern room and focuses the light
to warn the ships of dangers near the cliffs throughout the night.
He powers up the foghorn so to keep them all at bay
and knows they will be safe until tomorrow's break of day.

21 February 2021 [4]

Paul Gilliland

XXIV

A Snow Day
(Inverted Trochaic Sonnet)

Winter winds are freezing cold and blowing
all around the village where it's snowing.
Melting snow is dripping from the roof top;
icicles all hang like frozen fountains.
Dad is busy shoveling the blacktop,
piling up the snow in frozen mountains.
Mom is with the neighbors making small talk.
All the little children playing outside
building snowy men along the sidewalk;
climbing up the snow piles for a sleighride
School and work are cancelled due to weather.
Traffic in the streets is such a melee.
Home is where the family must tether.
Here we spend this very precious snow day.

21 February 2021 [4]

XXV

Waves Against the Shore
(English Sonnet)

The waves of time each lap against the sand
as morning's sun sends rays to break the dawn.
The ebbing tide retreats away from land
until the flowing streams are all but gone.
The sands of time are born from jagged cliffs
that face the sea defiantly with grace,
for as the waves maintain their rhythmic riffs
they slowly wash the grains from on its face.
Crescendos of the surf come with the storms,
while freezing winds provide some added aid
eroding rock gives way to newer forms
til even newer forms begin to fade.
The waves continue beating at the shore
until the rocky cliffs are there no more.

26 February 2021

XXVI

Solace of the Lord
(English Sonnet)

Begin each day with God the Lord above.
Kneel down to Him three times in daily prayer.
Receive the light of His forgiving love
And in it may you find some solace there.
Open the book of God; take time to read
The holy scriptures given you to share.
Within these words you'll find your daily creed
And in it you shall find some solace there.
Ask God to care for you throughout your sleep,
As you place life within His hands and care.
For pray that in your death your soul he'll keep
And in it you may find some solace there.
Then bless the Lord in all the deeds you do,
For in this solace is his love for you.

1 March 2021

XXVII

The Ides of March
(Double Sonnet)

We sense uneasiness on March's Ides.
A cold easterly wind blows 'cross the plain.
The waxing crescent moon affects the tides
as evening gloam brings forth the scent of rain.
The waning winds of winter start to blow
while whipping over barren desert land.
The sky gets dark as winds begin to grow
as winters final onslaught is at hand.
We pray the cold will spare the budding trees
whose flowers bloomed on warmer sunny days.
While daggers of the cold stab with a freeze
that on all things creates an icy glaze.
The darkness of the night fills us with fear
that winter's final rath is most severe.

But as the day begins at break of dawn,
a calming warmth sweeps over all the ground.
The wicked gales of winter have withdrawn
as calming warmer breezes now are found.
The equinox is only days away
and winter now has shown his final cards.
Though on the Ides of March he did betray
to give a theme to sonnet hungry bards.
While some remember Caesar's final day
when those he loved betrayed his loving trust.
I make this dissertation to convey
the harshness of the winter's final thrust.
For as the frigid winter winds renew
we ask like Caesar of his friends, "et tu?"

16 March 2021 [2]

XXVIII

World Poetry Day
(Acrostic English Sonnet)

Without a world that's filled with verse and rhyme
Our lives would be a mediocre grind
Relating deepest thoughts our only crime
Lest we become intrinsically entwined
Devoted to our craft of choosing words

Perplexed to find the right poetic phrase
Our task has made us all a band of nerds
Each vowing with our voices to amaze
They say the pen is stronger than the sword
Remembering this caveat's a curse
Yet every line must strike the perfect chord

Determining the most in every verse
And in the end, we're warriors with a quill
Yet bound by muses to write against our will

21 March 2021 [4]

XXIX

The Compass Rose
(Vondel Sonnet)

The flowers of the north bloom green and white
and bloom in winter snow to our delight.
They give a touch of warmth to mountain air.
The flowers in the south bloom pink and red
and grow along the forest paths we tread.
Small blossoms with a hue beyond compare.
The flowers in the west bloom in the blues
with touches of some purple and chartreuse
as they stand out against the desert sands.
The flowers in the east bloom orange and gold
and are the greatest flowers to behold.
The colors that the royalty demands.
Created in the way each flower grows
is nature's own inspired compass rose

21 March 2021 [4]

XXX

The Astronomical Clock of Prague
(Eramonian Sonnet)

With Vanity on the far left with mirror in his hand,
a Greedy miser with his gold is there upon his right.
The Turk of Lust with mandolin there opposite doth stand
next to the skeleton of Death who's clad in bones of white.
The Clock of Prague so proudly stands for centuries times six.
The sun, the moon, and zodiac are what its face depicts.
We stand there every hour and we look up at the face
to watch the grand procession of apostles in a row
as they pass by the windows, all transgressions to erase
bestowing each a blessing on the people down below.

28 March 2021

XXXI

How Beauty Kept the Beast
(Eramonian Sonnet)

Belle kept the Beast locked up by night and brought him out by
    day
to do some simple side show tricks for anyone who'd pay.
She cursed him with a magic spell to keep him in his place
and fed him magic potions that disfigured form and face.
Then she would take the money that she made from him each
    day
to buy the finest clothes she found to wear out on display.
The people all assumed the Beast was keeping Belle detained
and threats he made to those she loved was why she thus
    remained,
but Belle, she played the victim and, in all reality,
the Beast was actually the one kept under lock and key.

30 March 2021

XXXII

All Aboard!!
(Collection of Eramonian Sonnets)

We're all aboard the clipper ship and ready to set sail.
We point the ship's bow windward, and we pray the winds
     prevail.
We hoist the massive mainsail as we hope to catch a breeze
and as the pipes play "Auld Lang Syne", we sail out to the
     seas.
We sail into the great unknown, a better life to seek
for scriptures tell us that the earth is granted to the meek.
We sailed across the ocean vast for over sixty days
until we reached a strange new world and learned the native
     ways.
We built a village on the coast and there we persevered.
A new republic soon was formed from what we pioneered.

Now all aboard the railroad, for the train will soon depart.
We're moving to the city so to make a brand-new start.
The rural life is not for us, the city we prefer
for here we'll build our fortune and our dreams we won't defer.
We're awed by all the city lights; that flash all through the night
and all the office buildings rising up 'til out of sight.
The people here are friendly, and they help us make our way.
We earn enough to pay our rent and make it day to day.
At last, we get a giant break discovering success
from all the different jobs we've done and knowledge we
     possess

We're seated on the aeroplane and backing from the gate.
Our move across the continent is something that can't wait.
We heard that life is better on the coast that's on the west
where warmer days of summer tend to be the very best.
My girl became an actress on a weekly T.V. show
while I worked as a drummer with a punk rock band I know.
The friendliness of those we met helped take away our fears
for everyone we seem to meet helped us with our careers.
We spent our nights in disco clubs and weekends at the shore.
Our lives had gotten to the point we asked for nothing more.

We climb aboard a rocket ship and blast off to the stars.
We're looking for some type of life on Jupiter or Mars.
Escaping from the atmosphere into the dark of space
we hope that those inhabitants aren't gone without a trace.
We look for newer places where we all can settle down
establishing a colony or form a Martian town,
but as we float in empty space not knowing where we'll land
we realize this trip to space may not be as we planned.
We harken back to simple days when family was near
but realize we've finally found the final space frontier.

30 March 2021 [4]

March Winds
By Winslow Homer
Published in <u>Harper's Weekly</u>
April 2, 1859

XXXIII

When March Winds Yield unto the April Sun
(English Sonnet)

When March winds bring to us the warming breeze
the plants emerge from winter's slumber sleep.
As leaves begin to sprout upon the trees
and willows near the pond begin to weep
the harshly blowing winter winds abate
for warm calm Springtime breezes now belong.
The silent forests patiently await
returning migratory birds in song.
The April sun now dominates the day
providing all with warmth needed to grow.
The herbs give off their fragrant sweet bouquet
as flowers in the beds begin to show.
We know the dawn of Spring as thus begun
when March winds yield unto the April Sun.

4 April 2021 [2]

XXXIV

The Marriage of Prince Charming
(Double Fourteener Sonnet)

As young Prince Henry reached the age in which he
    should have wed
his father sent a message out to fill the bridal bed.
But Henry wanted not a princess for her royal line,
instead to find a simple girl with love for him divine.
The King relented to the wish to make the Prince agree
and for a ball he sent out invitations by decree
for every single maiden in the kingdom to attend
in hopes that young Prince Henry find a girl that he'd
    commend.
That night the charming Prince met every maiden in the
    land
and fell for simple Ella as the one to take his hand,
but Ella left at midnight, running out she lost her shoe
and all that Henry had of her was one glass slipper clue.
So, Henry ordered all the guards to find the one who's
    heel
fit into the glass slipper thus the princess to reveal.

The guards, they traveled far and wide examining each
    foot
until they found poor Ella who was covered black with
    soot.
The slipper was a perfect fit, but how could this girl be
the one that charming Henry knew was bound to marry
    thee.
When Henry saw her, he then knew that she was who
    he'd seen
but little did the good prince know the Queen would
    intervene.
And so, the Prince and Ella set the date when they'd be
    wed
but then a premonition came from someone who was
    dead.
Now, Henry's mum, the Queen, had died when he was
    only five
but marrying a commoner was something she'd deprive.
And so, each night she filled his head with thoughts of
    deep despair
until at last the couple split and ended their affair.
So, since his mother disapproved, she reached out from
    the grave
into his dreams as he did sleep, the bloodline so to save

5 April 2021 [4]

51

XXXV

Homage to E A Poe
(Italian Sonnet)

I hear a constant heartbeat in my head;
insistent drumming as the raindrops fall,
and ticking of the clock out in the hall
that fills my mind with sounds of fear and dread.
I hear the sounds of night while I'm in bed;
the silent creeping creatures as they crawl.
"For Nevermore," a distant raven's call
with church bells as they peal to raise the dead.
A presence that I sense, but cannot see,
the pendulum marks time with every swing,
the bumps and creaks that give my soul a fright
as images that manifest in thee.
Through darkness, to my sanity I cling
on this and every dark and stormy night.

13 April 2021 [4, 6]

XXXVI

The Mistress of the Night
(English Sonnet)

As evening falls within the forest deep
the owl leaves her nest to hunt for prey.
Nocturnal is the schedule she must keep
since cuddled in her nest throughout the day.
She flies up to her perch on silent wing
and sits within the luminescent glow
with pupils wide she looks for anything
that moves upon the forest floor below.
In stealthy swoops she dives in a surprise,
with talons out she pins prey to the ground.
A deadly grasp has guaranteed her prize
and up with velvet wings she's nest ward bound.
With wings that give this bird her silent flight
she's come to be the mistress of the night

14 April 2021 [4]

XXXVII

A Day in Nice, France
(Eramonian Sonnet)

For times when I must clear my head and grant my soul
    some peace
I pack my bags and set my sights on France's town of
    Nice.
Each morning I am greeted by the sunshine off the sea
and find myself a table in the shade of the marquee.
I eat my morning breakfast on the seaside esplanade
before I take a daily stroll along the Promenade.
The morning air is filled with scents of lavender and
    thyme
and sounds of people laughing and the midday church's
    chime.
A lunch of Salad Niçoise and a viewing of Matisse
will end my day of pleasure and will set my mind at
    peace

15 April 2021

XXXVIII

My Thoughts of You
(English Sonnet)

My thoughts throughout the day are all of you.
From warmth you bring to me with sunny rays
that dry my tears as fresh as morning dew
and clear away my clouds on stormy days.
I hear your footsteps in the falling rain
and hear your voice in every robin's song.
Each morning in the nightingale's refrain
are memories that linger all day long.
Your spirit is a welcome nightly guest
that soothes my soul as I lay down to sleep.
It comforts me throughout my time of rest
reminding me of memories to keep.
I see your smile when I look to the moon,
for you were taken from this world too soon

16 April 2021 [4]

XXXIX

The Full Pink Moon of April
(Eramonian Sonnet)

As geese and ducks fly northward on their migratory quest
to reach the forest wetlands where thy make their summer nest
the warmer days of spring appear, and new growth is revealed
as phlox in shades of pink begins to bloom throughout the field.
The full Pink Moon at April's end has powers that possess
great strength and creativity that brings forth much success.
A nature walk will radiate with fragrant sweet perfume
as springtime flowers soon will burst in rainbow colored bloom.
The frogs in every marsh and pond will start their evening song
to let all nature's creatures know they're back where they
    belong.

20 April 2021 [2]

XL

Our Quest for Love
(Terza Rima Sonnet // DOnnet)

Icy winter snowstorms blow and torment
and from our daily energy consume
love is froze in ice at every segment.

The rays of heaven bring forth flower's bloom
but hope for finding love is soon undone
by springtime's work and tasks as lives resume

Summer's sun we hope will bring inclusion.
Earthbound souls grow deep with love's desire.
All we see is but a grand delusion

The falling leaves are piled into a fire.
Autumn hearts of men remain resilient,
though finding any love is proving dire

Thoughts that love be found are ever present
although the sands of time still don't relent.

30 April 2021

Paul Gilliland

XLI

The Fairy Folk on Beltane
(Fourteener Sonnet)

As evening falls on Beltane Eve the fairy folk appear
from in the grove of Hawthorns where they live through the
    year.
A May Bush would be covered with bright ribbons and with
    shells
and clooties would be offered at the Beltane holy wells.
Now garlands made of primrose, hawthorn, gorse, and
    marigold
are placed around the doorways and the sills of houses old.
The humans build great fires, the Aos Si so to please
and leave upon their doorstep food and milk so to appease.
The fairies dance in circles where the mortals dare not roam
while humans build great bonfires to sanctify their home.
These folk of fairy mounds who now amongst the mortals dwell
are fallen souls from heaven yet too good to go to hell.
The fairy folk will vanish as the sun comes into view
and leave a youthful potion in the Beltane morning dew.

30 April 2021 [2, 7]

58

Romeo and Juliet
Engraving Poster
1879

XLII

Romeo and Juliet
(Acrostic English Sonnet)

Remember dear Verona's tale of love
Of star-crossed lovers thus forbid to wed.
Musicians sing of youthful joy above
Except that in the end they're both misled.
Our bounty is as boundless as the sea,

A plague on both their houses thus is cast,
No Montague had made worms meat of thee
Death of Mercutio is not surpassed.

Jumped over garden walls for his love's sake
Until sweet Juliet appeared in one.
Let light through that dark lonely window break
It was the east and Juliet the sun.
Endured there never was a tale of woe
Than this of Juliet and Romeo

7 May 2021

XLIII

The Fairgrounds
(Acrostic English Sonnet)

The end of summer every county seat
Holds festivals to celebrate the yield
Exciting days when all the farmers meet

For sharing their success in farm and field
And each young boy brings forth his winning steer
Intent to show that he can raise the best
Recounting all his work throughout the year
God knows he put his hard work to the test
Retired women bring their best baked wares
Of fruit filled pies and homemade cakes galore
Undaunted by the neighbor's jealous glares
Not worried since they've done this all before
Determined as the autumn leaves descend
September brings the summer to an end

7 May 2021

XLIV

Sands Through the Hourglass
(English Sonnet)

Like sand that passes through an hourglass,
it seems that mortal life is measured thus.
We give in to this scheduled planned impasse
believing that it's age defining us.
But age is not a number on a scale
where we approach the limit at the top.
For staying young at heart, we will prevail
to live our lives with no intent to stop.
With every change in life there's a new start.
Each chapter of our lives brings something new.
Although with age comes knowledge to impart,
there also are more worldly things to do.
For in the end, we know not where or when.
So, flip the glass and start your life again.

10 May 2021

XLV

Gone Without a Trace
(Eramonian Sonnet)

One's life must be worth living, every day we do our best.
Our thoughts and dreams are shared and our opinions are
      expressed.
We try to make an impact on those people all around
with hopes that in our later years our names will be renowned,
but often we go daily with so few that recognize
the simple gestures that are made before their very eyes.
As artists, authors, poets, we create despite the cost
in hopes that in the future all our work will not be lost.
Like footsteps on the beaches that the wind and waves erase,
our artistry may in the end be gone without a trace

11 May 2021

XLVI

Poetic Inspiration
(Fourteener Sonnet)

Poetic inspiration comes to me from all around.
From stars high in the evening sky to flowers on the ground.
From trees whose limbs embrace my soul when I'm on daily
    walks,
to subjects that come up with friends within our daily talks.
While looking through a picture book a scene may catch my
    eye
or maybe it will be the shape of some cloud in the sky.
Sometimes it's in the words I read upon a roadside sign;
like it was written there for me by someone's grand design.
Sometimes the words pop in my thoughts as I lay down to bed
and as I start to fall asleep, they grow inside my head.
I may wake up within the night to jot a line or two
in hopes that in the morning it might give my thoughts a clue.
No matter where I find myself; at sleep, at work, or play
I find poetic inspiration all throughout my day.

16 May 2021

XLVII

Riparian Forest
(Acrostic Italian Sonnet)

Rejuvenating life along the shore
Invigorated with the morning dew
Providing shade to rivers passing through
And creatures who along the banks explore
Reflecting scenes like never seen before
Inspiring young poets with its view
As springtime flowers bloom in every hue
Neglected beauty one cannot ignore

For all who wander to explore this space
Or venture to discover distant land
Remembrance of these scenes will thus remain
Enduring memories that we retrace
Sustained against the drought the trees withstand
Til rivers run again with mountain rain

22 May 2021

XLVIII

A Drabble Sonnet
(Ten-line or Drabble Sonnet)

I strive to form a new poetic style,
a fresh idea based on something past.
I research poetry and then compile
a sonnet form where lines are all recast.
I want to make it shorter than are most,
instead of three quatrains there's only two.
But still it keeps the readers all engrossed
by rhyming lines, the way that Will would do.
The syllables and lines are ten by ten
with rhyming couplet closing out the end.

31 May 2021

XLIX

An Evening in Early June
(Eramonian Sonnet)

The evening night is quiet and the trees, they softly sway,
the balmy breeze, a reprieve, from the heat wave of the day.
The sparrows and the finches with the titmice and the doves
are nestled in their cozy nests in branches up above.
The stars all twinkle brightly in the darkness of the night
while June's New Moon has risen but is hiding from our sight.
From stars up in the heavens we perceive the slightest glow
illuminating objects on the forest floor below.
We sit now in the gloaming here beneath the swaying trees
and listen to the whispers of the balmy summer breeze

10 June 2021 [2]

L

The Journey of the Fool
(Spenserian Sonnet)

Your life is at a standstill, so it
   seems.
You're lost inside a foolish state of
   mind.
When focused on your deepest
   darkest dreams
you feel all hope is lost and you're
   confined.
Although you always seem to be
   behind
good fortune may be right around
   the bend.
For welcome change is there to
   lead the blind
that take the leap of faith to
   comprehend.
A loyal, faithful dog's your only
   friend
to share with you the challenges
   you face.
For your adventure will be in the end
the love of life that you shall thus embrace.
You may not know what suit is meant to rule
for you are on the Journey of the Fool

THE FOOL.

10 June 2021 [2]

LI

Beware the Magician
(Fourteener Sonnet)

Is all that is among you an illusion
   or the truth
from stories once related to you in
   your years of youth?
There's magic all around you and
   your limits have no bounds,
but truth between the spirits and
   the living still confounds.
Magicians come to help you and
   to manifest your goal
and give restrained potential your
   unlimited control.
With purity of heaven and the
   knowledge of the earth
they help to guide your
   conscience in determining
   your worth.
By sparking creativity in finance
   and career
they take away the worries from
   the changes that you fear.
This power must be something that you shan't choose to abuse
for Masters of Illusion have some tricks meant to confuse.
Be mindful of your wishes and desires to compel.
No changing incantations once Magicians speak their spell.

11 June 2021 [2]

THE MAGICIAN.

LII

The Hierophant
(Acrostic Drabble Sonnet)

High Priest or Pope, just call it
what you will

Instilling values and morality

Eternal teaching staying with you
still

Reminding you of your mortality

On other hands it guides you by
decree

Perhaps to listen to your inner
voice

Habilitate to set your conscience
free

And make decisions benefitting
choice

No better understanding then of
course

To transfer knowledge from a trusted source

11 June 2021 [2]

LIII

The Guiding Star
(English Sonnet)

THE STAR.

A maiden kneeling by a blue
    lagoon
with stars aglow high in the skies
    above.
Bizarre a scene for in the
    afternoon
while in a nearby tree is perched
    a dove.
Two jugs of water held, one in
    each hand
are poured onto the ground and
    in the pond
with chakras all aligned we
    understand
the best is yet to come from the
    beyond.
So, make a wish upon these
    evening stars.
The lights that shine bright from
    the tunnel's end.
With hope that inner strength will soon be ours
as inspiration in your thoughts transcend.
Abundance in the world is at your side,
thus, let the Tarot Star become your guide.

12 June 2021 [2]

LIV

The Warrior in the Chariot
(Vondel Sonnet)

The Chariot with warrior standing
   tall
will signal you the victor over all.
With clear intention and a focused
   scheme
it's all about a forward moving will
of self-determination mixed with
   skill
for you to realize your lifelong
   dream.
Relationships for you are moving
   fast.
Establish future plans to make
   them last.
A strong foundation's needed to
   begin.
Do not let challenges impede your
   goal.
Your confidence must stay in your
   control
for you must have the willpower to win.
For now's the time to use all you possess
to turn career and love into success.

22 June 2021 [2]

LV

The High Priestess
(Terza Rima Sonnet)

The time has come for you to
    look within
for truth, first clear your mind
    then ask your heart.
The guidance that you seek is
    thus herein.
So, heed to what the spirits doth
    impart
for intuition is a better guide
to find the answers this is where
    to start.
Trust in the path your conscience
    will provide.
The moon illuminates the
    darkened mind
to knowledge that is already
    inside.
With harmony and balance now
    aligned
the truth within your soul will lead
    you to
emotional enlightenment enshrined.
The answers to your questions now await.
Just trust your instincts, they will guide your fate.

26 June 2021 [2]

LVI

The Moon
(Italian Sonnet)

Within the deck the eighteenth
    card's the Moon
that signifies illusions and your
    dreams.
Illuminating darkly hidden
    schemes
by bringing all disharmony in tune.
A long uncertain journey's
    opportune
on winding roads when guided by
    moon beams.
For hidden truth in life's not what it
    seems.
Deception in your job may come
    forth soon,
confusion and anxiety may grow
between the wild and docile sides
    of life,
but trust your intuition as a guide
for it will show you what you need
    to know
to help eliminate your daily strife
and see the truths that you have been denied.

4 July 2021 [2]

LVII

The Sun
(Brisbane Sonnet)

THE SUN .

The Sun puts freedom now in
    your control
for hard times never last beyond
    the dawn.
When opportunities are brought
    in view
the positivity to reach your goal
is strengthened by the trials
    undergone
and all the darker times that
    you've been through.
The sunny skies ahead will clear
    the gloom
for optimism's guiding your
    success.
The spontaneity that you provide
with warmth and happiness that
    lights the room
renews your passion and relieves
    love's stress.
For innocence shows nothing's there to hide
with clarity emerging in the light.
The other side of things is looking bright.

5 July 2021 [2]

LVIII

The Hanged Man
(Eramonian Sonnet)

The Hanged Man is inverted, his
    perspective now anew.
His dreams and his illusions seen
    from different points of view.
Suspended in reflection with his
    progress standing still
he's stuck within a waiting game
    with only time to kill.
With spiritual enlightenment to
    guide his inner thought
he sees through shifting shadows
    all the answers that are
    sought.
Surrendered to what's happening
    and pausing to reflect
accepting loss for greater good
    will set his quest correct.
For being stuck in limbo hanging
    from a tree up high
will guide him down a different
    path that is less traveled by.

9 July 2021 [2]

LIX

Summer Nights
(Jeffreys Sonnet)

I watch the stars come into view
with every evening night anew
while in the east the moon doth rise
and as the night gets ever dark.
The stars across the sky embark
upon their westward route reprise.
Before my eyes, the bright moon glow
enlightens all the world below
with luster shining through the trees.
With pensive thought I lay below
the ever-changing nightly show.
Accompanied by summer breeze
these times I seize without regret.
Forgetting not the nights like these.

10 July 2021 [2]

LX

Evening Skies at Twilight
(Sonnet Form 28)

The evening skies approaching twilight
come to view
in shades of blue
with setting sun in golden highlight
thus comprise
the evening skies.
Before our eyes with darkness looming
skies of blue
are changing hue.
With dark of night that's all consuming
stars arise
before our eyes.
The evening skies in shades of blue
Before our eyes are changing hue

13 July 2021

LXI

The Evening Breeze
(Sonnet Form 28)

The evening breeze ever so lightly
gently flows
in soft repose
and rustles leaves so ever slightly
in the trees.
The evening breeze.
From the seas the wind severely
stronger grows,
intensely blows,
and brings the sandy shores austerely
to their knees.
From the seas
The evening breeze in soft repose
from the seas intensely blows.

13 July 2021

LXII

Strength
(Kyrielle Sonnet)

Your intuition you shall heed
The heart is where your
    power's from
With fortitude your life is freed
To have the strength to
    overcome
For with the purity of heart
The positive results become
Successes in your life that start
To have the strength to
    overcome
The confidence to face your
    fears
Is key to great careers in some
While taking time to help your
    peers
To have the strength to
    overcome
Your intuition you shall heed
To have the strength to
    overcome

15 July 2021 [2]

LXIII

The Scales of Justice
(Reflective Sonnet)

With justice, fairness comes
    in all disputes.
In falsehood there is truth
    that it refutes
to bring forth harmony in all
    pursuits
restoring balance grounded
    in the truth.
The sword of truth is logic
    over heart.
In time the unknown truths
    with thus impart
the knowledge needed for a
    fresh restart
restoring balance grounded
    in the truth.
If you've been wronged by
    someone's evil deed
the balanced scales of justice
    intercede
reversing all the wrongs is guaranteed
restoring balance grounded in the truth.
For justice always guides us to the light
by balancing the wrong against the right.

15 July 2021 [2]

LXIV

July's Thunder Moon
(Occitan Sonnet)

The Buck Full Moon arrives in late July
as warmer summer days make antlers grow.
The corn is reaching high up to the sky
and berries on the bushes overflow.
The Thunder Moon brings lightning to the sky
with Jupiter and Saturn close in tow.
Lughnasadh's just a week away whereby
we reach the halfway point of summer's show.
A spiritual awareness with the moon,
connecting with one's truer, inner soul,
will bring the dissonance of life in tune
and grant authority and self-control.
For divination now is opportune
to bring the partial pieces to a whole.

16 July 2021 [2]

LXV

Temperance
(Onegin [Pushkin] Sonnet)

An angel guide's divine
    assistance
will forge the path for better
    health.
Have patience and deny
    resistance
with moderate approach to
    wealth.
Clear vision, patience, and
    persistence
when facing challenges
    existence
will set you on the proper road
with angel guidance thus
    bestowed.
The path of thoughtful
    moderation
is guided by the spirit plane
where peace and harmony
    maintain
a balance to the situation.
Cooperation is the key
with guidance from divinity.

17 July 2021 [2]

LXVI

The World
(Couplet Sonnet)

When life was at a standstill, so it
    seemed.
You focused on the things you only
    dreamed,
but perseverance guided you along
until your future confidence was
    strong.
The cycle now with harmony
    complete
will set the world of wisdom at your
    feet.
Success and victory will be
    received
as your life goals are set to be
    achieved.
You realize your deepest dreams
    came true
despite all of the trials you've been
    through.
Now finished is the Journey of the
    Fool
and you are now the person set to rule,
for now's the time to start a journey new
with knowledge you were able to accrue.

18 July 2021 [2]

85

LXVII

A False Hope
(English Sonnet)

The blue gray skies above are ominous
with evening air that's thick with scent of rain.
The storm clouds' growing size is monstrous
as they bring darkness all across the plain.
The rumble of the thunder in the east
with lightning bolts that brighten up the sky
bring hope the monsoon rain will be released
but then we see the storm begin to die.
As flashes of the lightning in the night
and thunder becomes few and far between,
the clouds begin to dissipate from sight
until the moon and stars are all that's seen.
And so, the waxing moon is shining high
above dry desert floors in mid-July

21 July 2021

LXVIII

The Ravaging of Mother Earth
(Golden Sonnet)

The world is faced with problems made by man
because he only cares about his own.
This was the case since all of time began
when he was placed upon the garden throne.
For centuries he's used without a plan.
Believing that the earth was his alone,
but as resources start to fade from view
he had no plan for how they would renew.
He rapes the earth of all she can provide,
then dumps his waste and smears it cross her face.
He wastes the precious resources supplied
until they all are gone without a trace.
And once all earth's organic life has died,
he looks for ways to ravage outer space.
Unless mankind will see things interlinked
he soon will find the human race extinct.

When looking at the fateful course of man,
the remedies to fix it are all known.
The question never has been if he can
or if the possibilities were shown.
The problem is he never made a plan
and now he's forced to reap what he has sown.
Acknowledging that truth can't be denied
for saving mother earth he must embrace.
He must let science be his basic guide
therefore, for man to save the human race.

22 July 2021

LXIX

The Ones Who Like To Stare
(Acrostic English Sonnet)

Outside the house I stay in shadows dark
Pretending to the world I am unseen
How different are times when I embark
To blend in with the crowd is my routine
Hallucinations vivid in my mind
Are always playing tricks with what I see
Like people staring at me from behind
Moreover, those who will not let me be
Objectives I can see within their eyes
Pretending to not glance and look my way
However, their demeaner shows the lies
Of all the views of me that they survey
Beware of all the people everywhere
Especially the ones who like to stare

*Ophthalmophobe – A person with a fear of being seen or stared at
    by others.*

23 July 2021

LXX

The Music of the Rain
(Spenserian Sonnet)

I wake up to the pitter of the rain,
the patter as the droplets hit the ground.
It's steady with a rhythmical refrain
as it continues falling all around.
My mind absorbs the gentle, soothing sound;
a hypnotizing mood that is serene.
The overcoming feeling is profound
as falling rain creates a tranquil scene.
I hear a far-off rumble in between
that adds intrigue within my daily dream.
Then lightning flashes suddenly are seen
that bring a climax to the nature theme.
The music of the rainstorm takes away
all worries that I had about today,

24 July 2021 [2]

LXXI

The Conjunction of the Moon with Jupiter and Saturn
(Spenserian Sonnet)

The rain had ceased, and clouds cleared from the sky.
The night was dark, and stars began to show.
The waning gibbous moon was rising high
providing luster to the ground below.
So, there within the moon's bright ivory glow
is Jupiter, illumined in the night
and further west sets Saturn in the row
defining moon's marked pathway to the right.
The eastern sky is lit with steady light
from these three bodies bright celestial scene.
Creating an extraordinary sight
as they all meet in space to reconvene.
Is this conjunction now an omen sent
or just some random heavenly event?

26 July 2021

LXXII

August's Blue Sturgeon Moon
(Eramonean Sonnet)

The full moon late in August is third of four this season.
The almanac states it is blue for this very reason.
It passes under Jupiter as it is on its route,
then Saturn is the next in line in its nightly pursuit.
The sturgeon of the Great Lakes living over seven score
have been traced back in time a hundred million years or
    more.
Due to the full moon's gravity that causes higher tide,
the bigger fish swim inland where small prey thus reside.
The fisherman will take this chance to catch the larger
    fish
at least that is the daily prize of every angler's wish.

21 August 2021 [2]

LXXIII

The Evening Sun
(English Sonnet)

The setting sun behind the mountain peaks
has lit the deep blue sky above ablaze.
With orange and yellow rays, the sunset streaks
across the sky in radiant displays.
Within a field, the flowers slowly sway
in rhythm to the softly blowing breeze.
They know that at the ending of the day
the temperature will drop a few degrees.
Within the distant farmhouse on the hill
a family gets ready for the night.
Expecting it will not be long until
the rays of sun have faded out of sight.
For as the setting sun drops out of view
the sky's awash with gold in every hue.

25 August 2021

LXXIV

Autumnal Equinox
(English Sonnet)

For as September's month comes to a close
and chilly breezes fill the atmosphere,
the time is now as everybody knows
to harvest crops, as fall is finally here.
With days becoming shorter one by one
allowing for the cooler nights to thrive
and with the slow descending of the sun
we know that turning leaves will soon arrive.
Bavarians have their Oktoberfest
while Mabon is the Pagan holiday.
They offer thanks for crops that they've been blessed
much like America's Thanksgiving Day.
Whatever holiday you celebrate
a wish that it will always turn out great.

19 September 2021 [2]

LXXV

The Demons in My Dreams
(English Sonnet)

As darkness falls, I fight to stay awake
for fear that demons haunt my nightly dream
and death arrives, my mortal soul to take
with torture 'til my inner voices scream.
I shiver in a pool of cold wet sweat
and feel my heartbeat pulsing in my head.
The horrors that I see I shan't forget
when in the darkness I lay down in bed.
I gasp for breath, anxiety takes hold,
it paralyzes me with fright and fear.
I feel that I am under the control
of creatures that in day do not appear.
If I can only dream within the light,
then how shall I find rest throughout the night?

11 October 2021 [6]

LXXVI

A Soldier's Heroic Crown Sonnet
(English Heroic Crown Sonnet)

1

As I began this tale in sonnet form
of those heroic men of years gone by,
I spoke of all the deeds they did perform
and sacrifices we could not deny.
What love does man hold dear above his life
that he would dedicate himself for thee
above his sons, his daughters, and his wife
to thus ensure that future men live free?
These brave young men who volunteer to serve,
who give their life for such a greater good,
for liberty they die so to preserve
a Constitution rarely understood.
For why one lays his life down for a friend?
It's often hard for some to comprehend.

2

It's often hard for some to comprehend,
for plots are often twisted with surprise.
But knowing of a life lost by a friend,
the actions of his life I must reprise.
Though with some women he had learned of love
or more perhaps the pleasure found in sex,
commitment was not what he sought thereof,
not falling under any woman's hex.
For he was satisfied to share his life
in service for the betterment of man
and thus had no desire for a wife
for that was never in his lifelong plan,
but as his life had started to reform
I saw the message of his tale transform.

3

I saw the message of his tale transform
as I began to see deep in his soul.
For in his mind there stirred a constant storm
of which he seemed to have no known control,
As governments declare that countries are
a detriment to life as we now know,
it's in the eyes of soldiers that are there
who shan't see foreign citizens as foe.
For people all throughout the world have needs
to live their life in peace and harmony
and we should never blame them for the deeds
of evil ones in the minority.
To make things right I hereby recommend
to understand the life of my dear friend.

4

To understand the life of my dear friend
I had to see the truth that he revealed,
for he had said "right" often did depend
on things that in the open were concealed.
He told me once that battles are not fought
by those who make decisions for a war,
but rather by the ones who have been taught
that there is more to life worth fighting for.
For it is just the young they send to fight
that suffers from the trauma he endures,
while politicians watch to their delight
the public's loud opinion reassures.
To make your choice this story will unfold.
This tale of one heroic man of old.

5

This tale of one heroic man of old
has long been kept in secret thus is said,
but now the time has come that it be told
in hopes that through the land his tale will spread.
A young man with wild dreams and high ideals
set off to join the army in his prime.
For honor, glory, liberty appeals
to those who see a mountain there to climb.
At first, they're smitten by romantic dreams
of grandeur as they face a faceless foe,
but battles aren't romantic, so it seems
when bullets end the lives of those you know.
But honor will not make the tears decrease
when giving all to bring forth worldly peace.

6

When giving all to bring forth worldly peace
he saw the frightened faces of the foe
and no sane way to conjure the release
of conflict that his heart had come to know
and so, throughout the years this struggle grew,
beginning to infest his conscious thought
'til it was hard to see which facts were true
and if these wars were simply all for naught,
but yet he held on to his firm belief
that leaders had an unseen master plan.
For in the end, it would relieve his grief
by warranting the righteousness of man.
But after years the truth would thus unfold
as stories long forgotten were retold.

7

As stories long forgotten were retold
in hopes that man would learn from days gone by,
but yet it seems those stories where controlled
and what was told was often just a lie.
They say the victor writes the history book
and thus, their point of view is kept alive,
however, it may mean that we've mistook
for fact the written fiction they contrive.
With truth erased the masquerade goes on,
true faces hidden underneath the masks,
as future generations thereupon
are asked to undertake aforesaid tasks.
The spinning carousel of life must cease
to see the violence all around decrease.

8

To see the violence all around decrease
we must treat every neighbor as a friend.
For only love can give us the release
to open up and truly comprehend.
Our inner soul does best when it's at peace,
a long life comes from laughing and from smiles.
For only when all wars and battles cease
can man appreciate the different styles.
Perhaps the cost of conflict is the bane
that keeps the global finances in black.
Large armies now each country must maintain
ensuring that no others will attack.
For hidden in the darkness of the night
the enemies know not those whom they fight.

9

The enemies know not those whom they fight,
there is no face of which to recognize.
Attacking from the shadows out of sight
relying on the aspect of surprise.
For meeting opposition face to face
can add a human factor to the game.
By showing some compassion in this case
may indicate that we are all the same.
For what about each other do we hate?
Does innocence mean anything in war?
This moral question's subject for debate,
an answer each man's conscience must explore.
For we would choose between what's right and wrong
if every person could just get along.

10

If every person could just get along
the world would be a better place indeed.
So, when in history did it go wrong?
Was it because of power or for greed?
Did people fear those different than them,
were they afraid of how their lives might change
and so, those that they feared they would condemn,
convincing all the others they were strange?
They caused division all throughout the land
with neighbor hating neighbor for a lie.
As rulers forced each one to take a stand,
it's very few that ever asked the "Why."
And as they add the fuel to the fight,
within each quest there is a path to light.

11

Within each quest there is a path to light
that opens up the soul to all things true.
We all are made aware of this despite
the trials that each man must first pass through.
For we must learn to show ourselves respect
and love oneself above all other things.
Alone this has an altering effect
with clarity that to our being brings.
This sense of peacefulness within our heart,
a calming aura that engulfs our soul.
The knowledge that the ancients do impart
are qualities that make our spirits whole.
They guide us down a path that can be long
where thoughts of every person can belong.

12

Where thoughts of every person can belong,
opinions of all people can be heard.
Together there is one voice loud and strong,
when open-mindedness is what's preferred.
But when the voice of some is drowned out
by those who still refuse to compromise.
Attempting to be heard they start to shout
and dark misunderstandings start to rise.
If only everyone would realize
that in the end we all have the same goal:
To live in harmony is for the wise
when every part contributes to the whole.
We find that compromise will not offend
if we can see each other as a friend.

13

If we can see each other as a friend
the conflict in your life will be reduced.
Although your way of thinking you defend,
ideas new to you are introduced.
You always need to keep an open mind.
Another's thoughts have merit as do yours.
And if the thoughts of both can be combined
it may not lead us to so many wars.
Whenever you are in a foreign place
beware of wolves that wear a lamb's disguise.
The truth is shown within a person's face,
the window to the soul is in their eyes.
For if we treat each stranger as a friend
we now can bring this cycle to an end.

14

We now can bring this cycle to an end.
I'll tell you now of how my hero died.
It was not in the ways that Fates intend
but rather in a way that he'd decide.
You see, his mind was full of lasting grief
of horrors he had seen because of war.
For orders contradicted his beliefs
but yet there was no way he could ignore.
As he looked in the other people's eyes,
he took and put the gun up to his head.
His conscience led him to his own demise
as he then took his own flawed life instead.
For he had seen the enemy transform
as I began this tale in sonnet form.

15

As I began this tale in sonnet form
It's often hard for some to comprehend.
I saw the message of his tale transform
to understand the life of my dear friend.
This tale of one heroic man of old
when giving all to bring forth worldly peace,
as stories long forgotten were retold
to see the violence all around decrease.
The enemies know not those whom they fight,
if every person could just get along,
within each quest there is a path to light
where thoughts of every person can belong.
If we can see each other as a friend
we now can bring this cycle to an end.

17 October 2021

Paul Gilliland

LXXVII

October's Full Hunter Moon
(English Sonnet)

October's Hunter Moon has risen high
as clouds are drawn like curtains made of lace,
where in the dark and gloomy autumn sky
they hang across the Blood Moon's shining face.
But still, it shines with bone white piercing glow
that brings good energy to start anew.
Providing light unto the earth below
that brings the fattened game more into view.
For as the chill of night falls on the ground,
preparing for the winter's task is here.
The Hunter's Moon in Aries is profound
when things no longer needed disappear
and as the moon climbs higher in the sky
the veil of clouds has bid the night good-bye.

20 October 2021 [2]

LXXVIII

The Celebration of Samhain*
* Pronounced "SAH-win"
(English Sonnet)

The veil between the realms is growing thin
as spirits of the dead prepare to rise.
On Samhain* they will come to visit kin
as living folk wear costumes for disguise.
We honor those departed with a feast
to share between the living and the dead,
but since through years the Christian faith increased
we celebrate All Hallows' Eve instead.
From singing songs in costume door-to-door,
receiving cakes and other morsels sweet,
we now have children dressed up as before
in what we now all know as Trick-or-Treat.
For some Samhain is faced with fear and dread,
for some a celebration of the dead.

29 October 2021 [2, 6]

LXXIX

An Autumn Night
(Terza Rima Sonnet)

The chilly autumn air blows through the night
as to the west the sun drops from our view.
The moon and stars provide the only light
as leaves all change into their autumn hue.
Within the forest trees deciduous,
they fill our minds with thoughts of déjà vu.
We lay here under heavens grand abyss,
the scent of burning wood wafts 'round our head
mixed with the smell of pine we can't dismiss.
The falling leaves in yellow, orange, and red
create a mattress underneath the trees
that now becomes for us a forest bed
and with the cooler freshness of the breeze
we learn that autumn truly does appease.

5 November 2021 [2]

LXXX

The December Sky
(English Sonnet)

With Jupiter and Saturn in our view
they're joined by Venus to provide us light.
They form a line to pass us in review
while much of our own moon is out of sight.
The hunter rises in the eastern sky,
his faithful canine always close behind.
The twins are standing to the left on high,
a bull is slightly further intertwined.
The planets and the constellations all,
a cosmic almanac on grand display
that foretell of the final days of fall
as we approach the yuletide holiday.
And as the nightly temperatures decline
the astral orbs shine forth in grand design.

5 December 2021 [2]

LXXXI

December 2021's Planetary Alignment

(Iambic Tetrameter Couplet Sonnet)

An astral alignment has come
on twelve December twenty-one.
As planets five form in a line
by astronomical design
They're joined there by our only moon
that will in time pass by too soon
and asteroids that number two
as Comet Leonard comes in view.
We ask them why they share their light
upon this most auspicious night.
Is this an omen; bad or good
of something we've misunderstood?
Or is this simply just a case
of how things are in outer space?

12 December 2021 [2]

A Heroic Crown and Other Sonnets

The Tropical Zodiac Sonnets

LXXXII

Aries
The Ram *(I am)*
(English Sonnet)

With Aries comes the rebirth of the spring
as Solis enters vernal equinox.
This fire sign, the flower blossoms bring
from daffodils to fields of creeping phlox.
The Arians love challenges and zest.
They're generous, courageous, and alert.
Beware, they are not easily impressed
but sensitive and really love to flirt.
They love to give and work for what they earn.
They're shy, in truth, a closet introvert.
Intelligent, recalling all they learn
they'll let you know if they feel they've been hurt.
They do the best with Centaurs and with Twins.
Aquarians and Lions for the wins.

31 December 2021 [2]

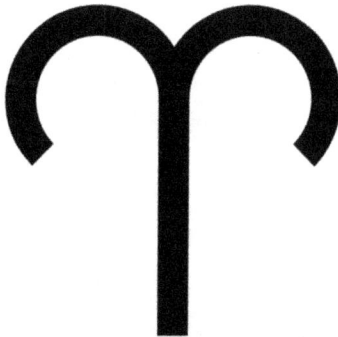

LXXXIII

Taurus
The Bull *(I have)*
(English Sonnet)

The Bull is next to grace the evening sky
while grounded with the element of earth.
It's ruling planet, Venus, is thus why
the Taureans crave the finest things from birth.
The outward show of wealth is their true call
and they can be a most eccentric host.
Their bed is what they cherish most of all
for sleep, is what the Bulls desire most.
Although their most discriminating quirk
may seem that they're extravagant or strange,
they are the most reliable at work
and dislike taking risks that cause a change.
With grounded signs they're best to interact
and Scorpio proves opposites attract.

31 December 2021 [2]

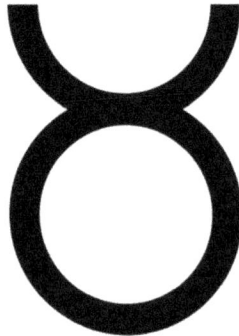

LXXXIV

Gemini
The Twins *(I think)*
(English Sonnet)

Now Gemini, the twins, are two-in-one
and rarely like to spend their time alone.
They need their other half to get things done
and wish that they themselves would be their clone.
They're longing to experience all lands
which fascinates their ever-changing minds.
Their intense curiosity demands
that they make different friendships of all kinds.
They're in this world to make it turn out right.
They'll give their life for brother or for friend.
The Gemini find love through words despite
the touch of their true partner in the end.
They get along with an Aquarian
or maybe with a Sagittarian.

31 December 2021 [2]

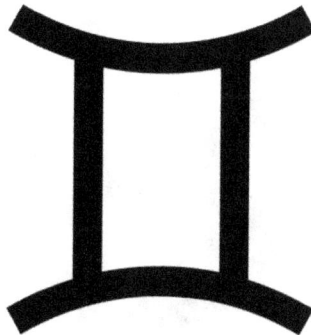

LXXXV

Cancer
The Crab *(I feel)*
(English Sonnet)

A Cancer is compassionate and kind
and lives its life between the shore and sea.
It's in the home where you will no doubt find
the most secure place for the crab to be.
Although it has a hard external shell,
it strives for loving households without strife.
Their loyalty to those close will foretell
that, once a friend, they are a friend for life.
They're often hard to deeply understand,
but family's the first thing they defend.
They're always quick to lend a helping hand
and do enjoy a good meal with a friend.
The Earth and Water signs they find sincere
while Air and Fire signs best disappear.

31 December 2021 [2]

LXXXVI

Leo
The Lion *(I will)*
(English Sonnet)

The Lion's heart is warm in life and love.
Achieving all things to which they commit.
They're passionate and generous above
the arrogance that makes them seem unfit.
They love to laugh and have a pleasing time.
Expensive things and holidays a must.
They're dominant and feel they are sublime
with many friends they're ones that you can trust.
Courageous and adventurous is why
the jungle king's innately born to lead.
Influenced by their charm one can't deny
to give the Leos everything they need.
The Centaur will fulfill its wildest dream
and Libra, Ram, and Twins all rank supreme.

31 December 2021 [2]

LXXXVII

Virgo
The Virgin *(I analyze)*
(English Sonnet)

A Virgo is intelligent and kind.
They're loyal, introverted, and demure.
At times somewhat judgmental and inclined
to find a pattern where is it obscure.
Perfectionists in all the things they do,
they have an eye for detail in each task.
With any job they're sure to see it through
while helping any friend with what they ask.
They're rarely motivated by their own
self-interest; more supportive of their friends.
They like to work on projects all alone
to fix a mess and tie up all loose ends.
The Fish or Crab are fine beyond compare.
Avoid the signs of Fire and of Air.

31 December 2021 [2]

LXXXVIII

Libra
The Scales *(I balance)*
(English Sonnet)

A Libra looks for balance in all things
where justice and equality prevail.
Obsessed by all the symmetry it brings
with harmony that evens out the scale.
A Libra is a social butterfly,
they do not like to spend time on their own.
Avoiding confrontations, they rely
on gentleness, a trait for which they're known.
They're motivated by how they appear
and thus, surround themselves with works of art.
They find a balance within their career
and harmony within their partners heart.
For they do best with fellow signs of Air,
of Earth and Water signs they should beware.

31 December 2021 [2]

LXXXIX

Scorpio
The Scorpion (*I create*)
(English Sonnet)

The Scorpion seems calm and quite subdued,
but they're emotional down deep inside.
A fire sign is often how they're viewed
since their true motivations tends to hide.
They like to know the truth and know they're right.
They're fearless, passionate, creative, bold.
They play the game with cards to chest held tight
and they can tell when lies are being told.
Emotions, thoughts, and secrets go unseen,
but to the closest friends they will affirm
they like their home-life stable and routine
with lovers in a partnership long-term.
With Earth and Water signs it's safe to share.
Avoid the signs of Fire and of Air.

31 December 2021 [2]

XC

Ophiuchus
The Serpent-Bearer *(I heal)*
(The Thirteen Sign)
(English Sonnet)

Ophiuchus, the interpreter of dreams
is secretive, insightful; hates routines.
They live life full of passion to extremes.
They're driven to succeed, or so it seems.
They do not like authority or rules.
It's knowledge and it's wisdom that they seek.
They detest being treated like they're fools
or anything that makes them out as weak.
They love a life of peace and harmony.
Companionship of others all the time.
As lovers, they have passion naturally
and leave the home when early in their prime.
With Rams and Crabs and Scorpions they're fine,
though Lions, Bulls, and Virgins are malign.

31 December 2021 [2]

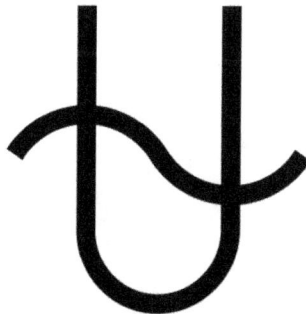

XCI

Sagittarius
The Centaur *(The Archer) (I see)*
(English Sonnet)

The Centaur is a warrior-poet sign
that seeks the truth where others dare not go.
Their quest for knowledge one cannot confine
for they desire everything to know.
They're outgoing with people that they meet.
The friendliest of all the party guests.
Their quest for knowledge never is complete
for life to them's a never-ending quest.
So, since this sign is always on the move,
the archer needs its space to freely roam
on thrill seeking adventures to improve
its understanding of things far from home.
The Ram and Lion love the jokes they tell.
The Virgin and the Fish don't work so well.

31 December 2021 [2]

XCII

Capricorn
The Sea Goat *(I use)*
(English Sonnet)

A Capricorn is practical and strong.
The hardest worker in the zodiac.
They need to feel like they in turn belong
and tend to strive where other people lack.
Methodical, well-organized, and wise
they like to follow rules that set controls.
Their eyes are always on the final prize,
they'll give up all they have to reach those goals.
They love to do improvements 'round the house
and party with a smaller group of friends.
They're loyal and supportive of a spouse
and strive to make things better in the end.
The Earth and Water signs are good-to-go.
The Air and Fire signs, best to say no.

31 December 2021 [2]

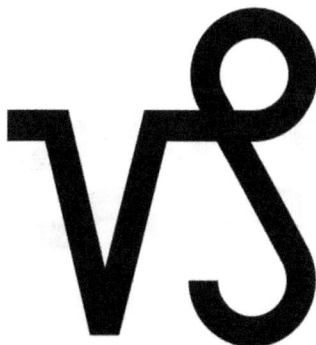

XCIII

Aquarius
The Water-Bearer *(I know)*
(English Sonnet)

Aquarians are sensitive and mild.
They want to make the world a better place.
Creative and inventive as a child,
it's forward-thinking aspects they embrace.
Their vision is the future will be bright
and freedom will be shared by everyone.
They strive that every soul is treated right
and drawn toward innovation that is fun.
Aquarians enjoy their time alone,
but work well within groups that see their worth.
They're often lost in thoughts of the unknown
as they explore the wonders of the earth.
The Ram or Twins with them a pair doth make.
The Lion or the Bull's a huge mistake.

31 December 2021 [2]

XCIV

Pisces
The Fish *(I believe)*
(English Sonnet)

A Pisces is compassionate and wise
with gentle and artistic points of view.
The fact that they like water's no surprise,
but far-fetched thoughts and dreams they will pursue.
Fantastic dreamers and great poets make,
for their imagination can run wild,
but often their attention is at stake
between reality and things beguiled.
A pair of fish that swim two different ways
divided in their purpose on the earth.
Creative talent takes up most their days
but doubt their own intelligence and worth.
The Water signs or Taurus are all fine.
The Centaur and the Twins, best to decline.

31 December 2021 [2]

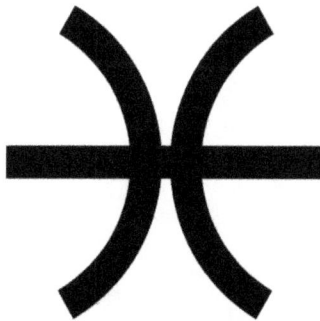

The Chinese Zodiac Sonnets

XCV

The Rat
(English Sonnet)

The Rats work hard to realize their goals.
They're charming and are quick to make some friends.
They're generally successful in their roles
but in regard to money, rarely lends.
They're outgoing and cheerful kind of folk
that get along with almost everyone.
When setting goals, they always go for broke
but rarely finish things that they've begun.
They live a thrifty life while working hard
and do well in a business of their own,
but lacks the courage to let down their guard.
Inquisitive, they question the unknown.
The Monkey, Dragon, Ox are best of course.
They should avoid the Rooster and the Horse.

31 December 2021 [2]

鼠

XCVI

The Ox
(English Sonnet)

The Ox works hard to pave successful routes.
It follows all procedures step-by-step.
It's diligent in all its work pursuits
but in relationships it is inept.
It has an eye for detail in each task
but small talk and large groups it does abhor
for being home is where it likes to bask
to execute each weekly garden chore.
The Ox has great endurance and respect.
It rarely loses temper and is kind.
It's self-opinionated and direct
and takes things slowly making up its mind.
We say it is as stubborn as an Ox
but gets along the best with Rats and Cocks.

31 December 2021 [2]

牛

XCVII

The Tiger
(English Sonnet)

The Tiger is competitive and brave.
They're confident; determined to succeed.
For power and authority, they crave
and winning is the motive that they need.
They have aggressive style like they are kings
but never will go back on what they say.
They need not plan for what the future brings
for they can handle all that comes their way.
They find it hard to make true lifelong friends
and married life for them can be mundane.
Their charm and generosity transcends
though ego and aggressive style remain.
A Canine, Horse, or Pig good partners make;
the worst would be a Monkey, Goat, or Snake.

31 December 2021 [2]

虎

XCVIII

The Rabbit
(English Sonnet)

The Rabbit is a tame and tender soul
both sensitive and honest to all ends.
Since leaving good impressions is its goal,
They're outgoing and popular with friends.
Conservative and cautious in its deeds
it dares not jump into a foolish act.
Considerate of all its lover's needs
with mystery that opposites attract.
A high sense of responsibility
and detail oriented to extreme.
Its business mind is one ability
that makes them awesome members of a team.
A Canine, Monkey, Pig, or Goat is great;
the Rooster or the Snake leave some debate.

31 December 2021 [2]

兔

XCIX

The Dragon
(English Sonnet)

The Dragon is a noble mythic sign,
mysterious and born with luck innate.
In truth, adventurous by its design
and wealth for them is easy to create.
The drive is strong to realize its dreams
with endless energy to reach success.
Though setbacks easily upset its schemes
which leaves the Dragon's will in grand distress.
A Dragon uses charm as its disguise.
Perfection's sought no matter what it takes.
They criticize the things that they despise
and won't admit when they have made mistakes.
The Monkey, Rat, or Rooster are the best;
the Oxen, Goat, or Dog's left for the rest.

31 December 2021 [2]

龍

C

The Snake
(English Sonnet)

The Snake is calm, perceptive, and is wise.
Its skill to make good judgements is its form.
Its thoughtful inspiration's no surprise
in chaos it's the center of the storm.
They often leave their future up to fate.
They're good at getting everything they thirst.
They're excellent seducers of a mate
in guarding them they're totally immersed.
A Snake will always want to get its way.
Be warned that you should never cross a Snake
or they will take revenge on you one day.
For you, that would become a huge mistake.
Although the Pig or Tiger may cause knocks;
they go well with the Monkey, Cock, or Ox.

31 December 2021 [2]

CI

The Horse
(English Sonnet)

The Horse is animated, warm, and kind.
It loves to be with friends and try new things.
At center stage its energy's refined
as to a crowd its entertainment brings.
They love to set themselves up on display
and work the best when placed on fast-paced teams.
They're masters of quick wit and repartee
who all believe in chasing after dreams.
The Horses love to travel and explore
in every culture they will prove adept.
Although they will seem faithful to the core
do not expect with them a secret's kept.
They should avoid the Snake, the Ox, or Rat;
a Tiger, Goat, or Dog is where it's at.

31 December 2021 [2]

馬

CII

The Goat
(Sheep / Ram)
(English Sonnet)

The Goat's imaginative, calm, and shy
and puts the needs of friends above its own.
Reserved and quiet is the reason why
with its own thoughts it likes to be alone.
Although they're good at making many friends,
they're sociable, considerate, and strong.
When spending time with groups it just depends
on whether they believe that they belong.
They seldom lose their temper or get mad
and have a love for children and the wild.
Their money's spent on things that are in fad
and on the finer things that they've compiled.
They do the best with Rabbit, Horse, or Boar;
the Tiger, Ox, or Dog they should ignore.

31 December 2021 [2]

羊

CIII

The Monkey
(English Sonnet)

The Monkey is intelligent and smart.
It's born with talents needed to succeed.
It plans to win before the races start,
becoming jealous when not in the lead,
They're innovative, humorous, and brave
and often face their challenges with schemes.
They're calm, collective thinking thus has gave
them aptitude to realize their dreams.
The Monkey folk prefer the urban life
with partners who can stimulate their mind.
Their use of clever jokes will cause them strife
although there's no intent to be unkind.
They do the best with Dragon, Rat, or Snake;
the Tiger or the Pig is a mistake.

31 December 2021 [2]

猴

CIV

The Rooster
(English Sonnet)

The Rooster is the favorite in a crowd.
Amusing for they love to entertain.
At times they can be arrogant or proud,
get cocky or appear like they are vain.
They're confident and always think they're right.
Observant and hardworking to a fault.
They're beautiful and always dress just right
and in their job, they're worth their weight in salt.
They're shrewd and optimistic and they do
just what it takes to get the things they need.
By working hard, they see the project through
for in the end, they know they will succeed.
With Dragon, Ox, and Snake we will endorse,
but cannot with the Rabbit, Rat, or Horse.

31 December 2021 [2]

雞

CV

The Dog
(English Sonnet)

The Dog is clever, honest, kind, and true
and to its friends is loyal and sincere.
It has a pessimistic point of view
not understanding things as they appear.
They're shy in social gatherings because
their thoughts are difficult for them to share.
They're sharp to criticize when seeing flaws
a vice of which they're often unaware.
It takes a while for Dogs to make a friend.
They tend to be distrustful at the start.
But once accepted, bravely will defend
and give to them their pure and faithful heart.
The Rabbit is considered best by far;
the Dragon, Goat, and Cock aren't up to par.

31 December 2021 [2]

狗

CVI

The Pig
(English Sonnet)

The Pig is loyal, honest, and naïve.
Regarded for the pureness of its heart.
Devoting all their vigor to achieve
the optimistic goals that they did start.
They'll sacrifice themselves for greater good.
They will not ever waiver or retreat.
For serving others, it is understood
and making friends with everyone they meet.
It's hard for them to detect those that lie
for they believe that every heart's sincere.
But falling victim to the rogues is why
they're forced to play the fool year after year.
The Rabbit, Sheep, or Tiger partners make;
best avoid the Monkey or the Snake.

31 December 2021 [2]

A Heroic Crown and Other Sonnets

CVII

February Snow Moon
(Spenserian Sonnet)

The full moon on a February night
has burned away the clouds once filled with snow
allowing it to share its evening light,
illuminating all things down below.
The fields and forests have a mystic glow
as branches cast their shadows in the gloam
that dance as evening breezes start to blow
and creatures of the night begin to roam.
As we retreat into our cozy home
and evening breezes quickly chill the air,
emerging from the trees the forest gnome
will venture out to offer up a prayer
for him and every other forest sprite
be granted strength and power on that night.

19 February 2022

CVIII

What Awaits Us in Death
(English Sonnet)

We live our lives in wonderment each day
of what tomorrow's fate will have in store
and trudge on with regrets of yesterday
as we pray that our future holds much more.
But with each passing week filled with regret
of hours in our lives we can't regain,
and fortunes built through years amassing debt
that in the end we learn was all in vain.
For when this life we've lived has duly passed
and from our mortal shell the soul's set free
we realize eternity is vast
and not how we expected it to be.
If we knew what awaited us in death,
would we then cherish or despise each breath?

20 March 2022 [10]

CIX

The Paschal Moon
(English Sonnet)

Behind the mountains rising in the west
the pink of dusk now fills the evening sky.
The sun retreats to take its nightly rest
as April's full moon shines down from on high.
Though veiled behind the gossamer of clouds
it glows within the fading gloam of night
to shine through all those wispy evening shrouds
and give a calming luster with its light.
The Paschal Moon that lights the holy days
when Jesus met his death and rose again
illuminates the hours of our praise
when he became the savior of all men.
For this full moon, the first one of the spring,
illuminates the glory of the King.

15 April 2022

CX

The Lonely Owl
(English Sonnet)

Within the shadows of the forest trees
the lonely owl perches in the night
as her soft feathers ruffle in the breeze
and shimmer in the dancing rays of light.
But then, as there is motion down below
she spreads her wings and glides in silent flight
with outstretched talons makes the fatal blow
so quick her prey cannot put up a fight.
Unto her nest she carries forth her prize
for hungry mouths wait silently to feast.
The prey hangs from her talons as she flies
until within her nest it is released.
The brood of owlets feed upon the kill
until each tiny mouth has had its fill.

24 April 2022

Explanation of Sonnet Forms

Basics of Sonnet Form

There are many variations of the sonnet form, however, traditional forms consist of a poem of 14 lines, with each line containing 10 syllables.

Most sonnets are written in iambic pentameter (five feet of iambic meter). Iambic meter consists of an unstressed syllable (u) followed by a stressed syllable (S). Therefore, iambic pentameter would read as "u S u S u S u S u S" as in William Shakespeare's famous opening line to his 18th sonnet –

Shall I compare thee to a summer's day?

The different variations of sonnets are often attributed to the rhyme scheme of the verse, as each variation will use its own unique rhyme pattern.

This collection of sonnets contains not only verse written in traditional sonnet forms, but also verse using more obscure sonnet forms. Each form used in this collection is briefly explained below.

Italian Sonnet (also known as a Petrarchan Sonnet) is credited to being invented by Giacomo da Lentini in the 13th century, this form was popularized by the Tuscan poet Francesco Petrarch who used the form to write love poems to a woman named Laura. Italian sonnets tend to be themed around love and nature.

The poem begins of two quatrains (stanzas consisting of four lines each) to make up a single eight-line stanza called an octave and ends with two tercets (stanzas of three lines each) that make up a single six-line stanza called a sestet. The standard rhyme scheme for the octave is ABBA ABBA while the rhyme scheme for the sestet is CDECDE.

Typically, the Italian Sonnet is divided into two parts: The octave is considered the "Proposition" which establishes a problem or question. This is followed by the sestet which begins with what is called the "turn" in the ninth line that sets up the final lines of the sestet as the "Resolution."

The Miltonic Sonnet is named after the English poet John Milton and uses the same rhyme scheme as the Italian sonnet, however, instead of dealing with themes about love or nature, as in the Italian sonnets, they address politics and moral issues.

Occitan Sonnet is a variation of the Italian Sonnet that dates back to the late 13th century. It employs a rhyme scheme that mixes the Italian and English sonnet forms – ABAB ABAB CDCDCD.

English Sonnet (Also known as an Elizabethan or Shakespearean Sonnet) was introduced to the English language by English poet Thomas Wyatt in the 16th century when he translated the works of Petrarch from Italian. Wyatt's contemporary, Henry Howard, Earl of Surrey, is credited with innovations to the sonnet form that became well known as the English Sonnet, a form popularized by the works of William Shakespeare.

The defining characteristic of this form is the use of three quatrains of four lines each followed by a two-line rhymed couplet. The rhyme scheme is ABAB CDCD EFEF GG.

Spenserian Sonnet is a 16th century variation of the English sonnet created by English poet Edmund Spenser using the rhyme scheme – ABAB BCBC CDCD EE.

Couplet Sonnet is a 14-line sonnet made up of seven sets of rhymed couplets. This is sometimes referred to as a Clare Sonnet after the English Poet John Clare (1793-1864). This form is closely related to the Welsh poetic form Cyhydedd Fer which consists of seven rhymed couplets. However, the Cyhydedd Fer is composed with rhyming eight syllable lines instead of the standard ten-syllable lines of a sonnet. The rhyme scheme of a Couplet Sonnet is AABBCCDDEEFFGG.

Fourteener Sonnet – In poetry, a fourteener is a line consisting of 14 syllables, usually consisting of seven iambic feet (also known as iambic heptameter) and commonly found in English poetry of the 16th and 17th centuries. Fourteeners often appear as rhymed couplets but can follow any sonnet rhyming pattern. A Fourteener Sonnet is a Couplet Sonnet consisting of 14 syllable lines, thus giving the poem a square form of 14 lines each consisting of 14 syllables. The rhyme scheme is AABBCCDDEEFFGG.

Eramonean Sonnet (Also referred to as an Inverse Sonnet) was developed by American poet Antonio Eramo in 2020 as an experimental poetic form. Where a traditional sonnet consists of 14 lines with 10 syllables per line, this sonnet form consists of the inverse, 10 lines with 14 syllables per line. The form was developed as two quatrains separated by a rhymed couplet. The original suggested rhyme scheme is ABAB CC DEDE, however, I determined that the use of rhymed couplets throughout had a better flow, thus the rhyme scheme of AABBCCDDEE. Both versions are represented in this book.

Drabble Sonnet – In literature, a Drabble is a story consisting of exactly 100 words and a Dizain is a French poetic form consisting of exactly 100 syllables. Although a Drabble Sonnet would be a sonnet consisting of exactly 100 words, I developed the Drabble Sonnet as the opposite of the Fourteener Sonnet discussed above, thus having a 10-line stanza with 10 syllables per line consisting of a total of 100 syllables as opposed to 100 words. A Drabble Sonnet can be based on word count and can follow any sonnet rhyming pattern. My Drabble Sonnet based on syllables follows a shorten English Sonnet form consisting of two quatrains followed by a rhymed couplet. The rhyme scheme is ABAB CDCD EE.

Dizain - A Dizain is a 15th and 16th century French poetic form also consisting of a 10-line stanza with 10 syllables per line, however, the rhyme scheme is ABABBCCDCD.

Terza Rima Sonnet – Terza Rima (translated to "third rhyme) is an Italian term for a poetic verse that uses an interlaced or chained rhyme pattern. The 14th century Italian poet Dante Alighieri is the first known poet to use this form in his epic poem <u>The Divine Comedy</u>. Later, Petrarch used this form in his works. The sonnet is made up of four tercets (three-line stanzas) with the first and third lines rhyming. The next stanza will use the second line of the previous stanza as the rhyme for its first and third lines. The fifth stanza will be a rhymed couplet using the rhyme from the second line of the fourth stanza. Therefore, the rhyme scheme for a Terza Rima Sonnet is ABA BCB CDC DED EE.

The DOnnet was developed as an experimental Terza Rima Sonnet form by American poet Antonio Eramo in 2021. The form is based on the four Taoist trigrams for heaven (☰), water (☵), fire (☲) and earth (☷) plus yin-yang. The solid lines represent a masculine (stressed) line ending and the broken lines represent

a feminine (unstressed) line ending. The couplet representing yin-yang (balance) has one of each.

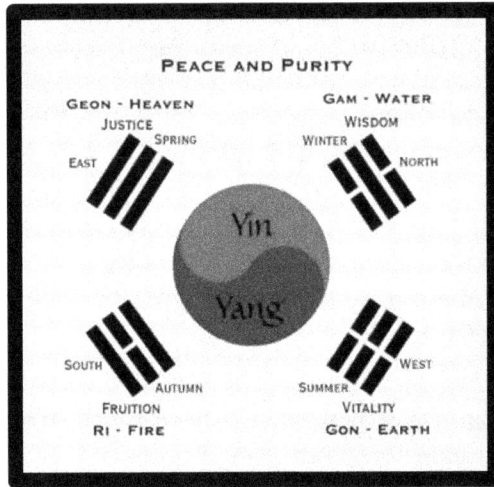

The masculine ending is indicated by an uppercase letter and the feminine ending is indicated by a lowercase letter. The rhyme scheme for this sonnet is ABA bCb CdC dad aA. The challenge to writing in this form is incorporating rhyming words with both masculine and feminine endings.

Acrostic is a poem in which the first letter (or syllable or word) of each new line spells out a word or phrase. An Acrostic Sonnet is simply a sonnet using any sonnet form where the first letter (or syllable or word) of each new line spells out a word or phrase related to the subject of the poem.

Vondel Sonnet is a 17th century sonnet form developed by Dutch playwright and poet Joost van den Vondel consisting of 2 sestets followed by a rhymed couplet. It employs the rhyme scheme of AABCCB DDEFFE GG.

Jeffreys Sonnet is a 21st Century variation of the Vondel sonnet created by American artist and poet Scott J. Alcorn, consisting of only eight syllables per line, two sestets, and ending with a cross rhymed couplet. The rhyme scheme appears as AABCCB (B)DDEFFE (E)G (G) E. (The letters in parenthesis indicate the cross rhymes).

Brisbane Sonnet is a sonnet consisting of two sestets and a couplet. The rhyme scheme is ABCABC DEFDEF GG.

Kyrielle Sonnet – A Kyrielle is a poetic form that originated in troubadour poetry with a repeated line or refrain at the end of each stanza and the first and last lines of the first stanza serving as the line of the closing couplet. It is generally written in iambic tetrameter (eight syllables per line). The Kyrielle Sonnet consists of three rhyming quatrain (four-line) stanzas and a non-rhyming couplet. It uses the rhyme scheme of AabB ccbB ddbB AB (or) AbaB cdcB dbdB AB (The uppercase letters indicate the positions of the repeated lines.)

Reflective Sonnet is a sonnet form developed by American Poet Courtney Glover that incorporates three tercets (three rhyming lines) each followed by a reoccurring refrain (R^1) and closing out with a rhyming couplet. Written in iambic pentameter. The rhyme scheme is AAAR^1 BBBR^1 CCCR^1 DD.

Iambic Tetrameter Sonnet – A sonnet form consisting of only eight syllables per line rather than the traditional ten. William Shakespeare used this form in his Sonnet 145.

Onegin Stanza (also known as a Pushkin Sonnet) is a poetic form popularized and possibly invented by the 19th century Russian poet Alexander Pushkin throughout his novel in verse Eugene Onegin. Like the English Sonnet, the poem can be divided into three quatrains with an ending couplet, however, the verses are written in iambic tetrameter with alternating masculine and feminine endings. The rhyme scheme is aBaB ccDD eFFe

GG. The lowercase letters represent the feminine rhymes (the stress falls on the penultimate syllable and each line has nine syllables) and the uppercase letters represent the masculine rhymes (the stress falls on the final syllable and each line has eight syllables).

Golden Sonnet is a sonnet form I developed in 2021 that utilizes the Golden Ratio to divide the two stanzas and provide the point for the volta (or turn) to occur. It is written in iambic pentameter and with two octets followed by a sestet and a quatrain. The rhyme scheme is ABABABCC DEDEDEFF ABABAB DEDE.

Inverted Trochaic Sonnet is another of my experimental forms that inverts and reverses an entire English Sonnet form. Each line is written in trochaic pentameter (trochaic is an accented syllable followed by an unaccented syllable). It begins with a rhymed couplet followed by three quatrains. The rhyme scheme is AA BCBC DEDE FGFG.

Crown of Sonnets (also known as a Sonnet Corona) is a sequence of sonnets usually addressed to a single person or concerned with a single theme where each of the sonnets explores an aspect of the theme. Each sonnet is linked to the succeeding sonnet by repeating the final line as the first line of the next sonnet. The final line of the final sonnet will be the first line of the first sonnet, thus bringing the sequence to a close. The sonnets can follow any know rhyme scheme and there is no known rule that each and every sonnet must be in the same sonnet form.

Heroic Crown (also known as a Sonnet Redouble) is an advanced form of a Crown of Sonnets, it is comprised of 15 sonnets which are all linked the same as in the Crown (last line of the 14th sonnet will be repeat the first line of the first sonnet.

The 15th sonnet is thus comprised of the first line of each of the preceding 14 sonnets in order and is called the Mastersonnet. This form was invented by the Siena Academy, which was formed in 1460, but there are no known existing crowns of sonnets written by them.

Form 28 Sonnet is a sonnet form developed by British poet James Khan in 2021. A 14-line poem consisting of both four and eight syllable lines, reoccurring rhymes, and repeated refrains. The poem is made up of four syllable phrases (although some occur in the same line to form an eight-syllable line) that break into two sestets and a rhymed couplet. The rhyme scheme is:

Rhyme	Syllables
A^1 / b	4 / 4
c	4
C^1	4
b	8
a	4
A^1	4
A^2 / d	4 / 4
C	4
C^2	4
D	8
A	4
A^2	4
A^1 / C^1	4 / 4
A^2 / C^2	4 / 4

Footnotes

[1] – Originally published in <u>Hindsights of 2020</u> (Paul Gilliland, 2021)

[2] – Originally published in <u>The Journey of the Fool – A Poetic Journey in Three Parts</u> (Paul Gilliland, 2022)

[3] – Compiled and edited by Paul Gilliland (Southern Arizona Press, 2022)

[4] – Previously published in <u>Sonnet Sanctuary Volume 1</u> (Romeo Nation, 2021)

[5] – Previously published in <u>The Poppy: A Symbol of Remembrance</u> (Southern Arizona Press, 2022)

[6] – Previously published in <u>Ghostly Ghouls and Haunted Happenings</u> (Southern Arizona Press, 2022)

[7] – Previously published in <u>Dragonflies and Fairies</u> (Southern Arizona Press, 2022)

[8] – Previously published in <u>Open Skies Quarterly, Volume Four</u> (Shrouded Eye Press, 2021)

[9] – Previously published in <u>Perceptions - Open Skies Collections</u> (Shrouded Eye Press, 2021)

[10] – Previously published in <u>From Sunset to Sunrise and Everything in Between</u> (Dark Poetry Society, 2022)

About the Author

Paul Gilliland retired after over 30 years of service with the US Army and settled in the high desert of Southeast Arizona, just miles from the historic wild west towns of Tombstone and Bisbee. He holds Associate of Applied Science Degrees in Intelligence Studies, Linguistics, and Education from Cochise College; a Bachelor of Arts Degree in Music Theory/Composition and Technical Theater Design from Olivet College; and a Master of Fine Arts Degree in Music Composition from the Vermont College of Fine Arts. He is an educator, composer of 21st century chamber music, author, form poet, and publisher. He is a member of the American Society of Composers, Authors, and Publishers (ASCAP); National Writers Union; Authors Guild; Poetry Society of America; the Academy of American Poets; and the Association for Publishers for Special Sales. In addition to teaching interviewing techniques and report writing for the US Army, he is the Editor-in-Chief of his own publishing company, Southern Arizona Press. He currently has two published volumes of poetry, *Hindsights of 2020* and *The Journey of the Fool: A Poetic Journey in Three Parts*, both available through Amazon and is currently working on completing his fourth collection of poetry, *Tales from a Southwest Inn*. His poetry appears online in numerous Facebook poetry groups as well as being published in *Sonnet Sanctuary Anthology Volume 1* (A Romeo Nation), *Open Skies Quarterly Volumes 4, 5, 6*, *Perceptions*, *Dark Reflections*, and *Myths, Legends, and Lore* (Shrouded Eye Press), and *From Sunset to Sunrise* (Dark Poetry Society Anthology).

He can be followed online at:

https://www.facebook.com/PaulGillilandPoetry
https://www.facebook.com/SouthernArizonaPress
http://www.PaulGillilandMusic.com/
https://www.SouthernArizonaPress.com/

www.ingramcontent.com/pod-product-compliance
Lightning Source LLC
Chambersburg PA
CBHW060800050426
42449CB00008B/1470